Les Demoiselles d'Avignon

Picasso

Les Demoiselles d'Avignon

A Sketchbook

Text by Brigitte Leal

Thames and Hudson

Editions de la Réunion des musées nationaux

Translated from the French
by Suzanne Bosman

Printed and bound in France

A Sketchbook for
Les Demoiselles d'Avignon

EYES BRIMMING OVER with sadness, a nose like a disfiguring scar, a body broken and deformed by a lifetime of ill-use . . . .

As soon as we open this sketchbook, the most striking image of *Les Demoiselles d'Avignon* confronts us, that of the head of the woman sitting on the right whose brutal formulation was to arouse so much controversy. This charcoal study is completely extraneous to the rest of the sketchbook in that it identifies with preliminary studies for the second state of the painting, the right-hand side of which was reworked during the summer of 1907. The rest of the book, however, relates, both in iconographical and in stylistic terms, to the first version of the painting roughly sketched out in the spring of 1907. Nothing, or almost nothing, was known of this first version, as indeed of the definitive one, until Picasso's death revealed the hidden treasures of his studios – the most precious perhaps being his sketchbooks, and especially the set of fifteen books of preparatory studies for *Les Demoiselles d'Avignon* which could now at last be seen as a whole.

This particular sketchbook remained unpublished for a long time (Christian Zervos reproduced a random selection of the best pages in 1973, the year of the painter's death) and it stands out as the finest flower in this suite of the artist's creative process. With its seventeen major compositional studies, it is the only sketchbook to contain all the characters that were to appear in the final work (the five women) together with the two additional women and the two men who were eventually to be dropped from the composition. Other images, which were later to disappear, find their place in these pages and their outwardly neutral appearance fails to disguise their highly symbolic quality – the bowl of ripe fruit, for example, or the bitch, Fricka, that Picasso owned.

The sense of mystery which has reigned over the history and meaning of *Les Demoiselles d'Avignon* was always carefully maintained by Picasso himself ('by negligence or perversity' on his part, Leo Steinberg suggests). Perhaps irrevocably offended by the harsh judgment made by the artists, art-lovers or friends who had the good fortune to see the painting in its definitive form in his Bateau-Lavoir studio in July 1907, and then irritated by the accusations which were made against him regarding his borrowings from African art, Picasso was from then on proudly to ignore all critical interpretations of the work. Only during a wonderful and moving conversation with André Malraux which was later reproduced in *La Tête d'Obsidienne*, published a year after the artist's death, did Picasso give some clue, once and for all, as to the true meaning of the work. In the course of this conversation, which took place in Paris one evening in 1937 while Picasso was finishing *Guernica*, he recalled his discovery of the ethnographical collections at the Musée du Trocadéro during the summer of 1907. . . . 'All alone in that awful museum, with masks, dolls made by the redskins, dusty manikins. *Les Demoiselles d'Avignon* must have come to me that very day, but not at all because of the forms; because it was my first exorcism-painting – yes absolutely!'

All alone. . . . What prompted Picasso, in this solitude, to embark, in the autumn of 1906, upon a large painting of nudes, as had Ingres and Cézanne before him, and as Matisse was then also doing?

In a large, rectangular sketchbook, bound along the shorter edge, exactly like this one, he began to draw standing female nudes from every angle. During the winter, he was still feeling his way, filling up the pages of a second sketchbook of nudes with well-rounded forms and rippling muscles, taking his time over the formulation of the faces with their unseeing eyes. Right in the middle of the sketchbook, a first compositional study appears, sketched rapidly, while the artist was still working out a composition – perhaps his first intention for the painting – consisting of two women facing each other in an interior hung with drapes, the folds of which he drew and redrew at length.

In March 1907, he had at last found his theme. He acquired a third sketchbook, the one which concerns us here, and he crammed its pages in less than a month, in order to evoke, as he explained later to Christian Zervos, 'the recollections of a Barcelona brothel in the rue d'Avignon' (i.e., the Carrer d'Avinyo).

Sheet after sheet, these recollections take form under our eyes, on pages at times furiously obliterated or even ripped out, crowded with corrections and revisions.

Legend, fuelled by the expressive intensity of the finished painting, would have us believe that Picasso conceived it quickly, painting directly on to the canvas as if possessed by a demonic rage. The great number of preparatory studies, both in the form of loose pages and oil studies, as well as the sketchbooks, serve to disprove this romantic theory. The drawings of this sketchbook also reveal that this masterpiece, which was matured over a long period, owes much to classical procedures – Jacques-Louis David's series of studies for his *Serment du Jeu de Paume* comes to mind. In the compositional studies, Picasso establishes the structure, placing the groups in a nervously calligraphic and spontaneous style, as if carried away by the torrent of ideas. Then a calmer style takes over, portraying each figure in isolation from every angle and, in the case of two of them, both naked and clothed. With rich and firm strokes, he carefully examines each image, refining a pose here, enriching the details of a hairstyle or a drapery there. He gives particular attention to the faces, which are increasingly seen in close-up, carefully delineating their contours with slight changes here and there to the shadows which model a cheek, to the tilt of a head or to the quality of a smile. . . . Even the humble flowers of the still-life with its rustic jug undergo this rigorous analysis.

These studies also reveal the conflicting ideas which reigned during the gestation of the work. Three sketches clearly show that Picasso was already thinking at this time of replacing the horizontal format, which would allow for a frieze-like composition, with a square one, emphasizing the vertical element which would favour a more compressed perspective.

The general structure, despite its complexity, seems to have sprung fully-fledged from the artist's imagination. On one page he first of all draws two sweeping diagonals right across the sheet which intersect slightly left of centre, and these give the general dynamic construction of the composition. Seven figures then take their place in the spaces made by the four resultant triangles, and the accentuated corner of the small, low table, borrowed from Ingres's *Bain Turc*, begins to intrude unsettlingly at the base of the composition. These triangles then transmute themselves into the gentler curves of heavy drapes which divide up the surface, framing it like a theatre stage and gathering up the figures tightly grouped in twos and threes in their folds – swollen folds which have a womb-like quality cushioning them from all interaction. For in this suffocating space, flesh touches flesh without eyes ever meeting. The greenhouse atmosphere of the *Bain Turc* is re-created by means of a theatrical staging, the baroque character of which Leo Steinberg has rightly pointed out. All over the stage, the characters take their place, one by one, forming a circle around a meagre meal. With a sharpened piece of chalk, the artist delineates some of the protagonists with a jagged outline, or with a fluid stroke suggests faceless, indeterminate figures which, little by little, will assume a human appearance.

Here and there, a pubic triangle, the twin curves of breasts and long hair tumbling down a back serve to denote a woman. On the other hand, two figures, one exactly in the centre of the composition as if transfixed to the corner of the table and the other in profile on the left, remain at an indeterminate stage until Picasso covers their nakedness with costumes which identify them as members of the male sex.

What else would one expect to find in the sitting room of a brothel but girls and their clients? Picasso is no Matisse who places his delicate odalisques in Arcadian gardens. Picasso's nudes, his 'bathers', are sexual beings and are not afraid to show it.

The girl squatting in the corner on the right is without doubt the most shameless, opening wide her thighs as though showing off her wares. The one opposite her, ensconced in an armchair with her legs crossed high is hardly more discreet. As for the caryatid who stands in a classical pose reminiscent of Michelangelo's *Slave* (of which Picasso was later to own a cast), she impassively displays her attributes with a nonchalant grace worthy of an Ingres. The two other women approach to draw aside the curtain in order to see the newcomer. Who is this man entering on the left with a book under one arm?

Indeed, this slightly embarrassed young man with his wide-open eyes, is an odd client. For he seems to be presenting a skull to our young ladies, who show their interest by turning their faces towards him. According to Picasso, he is a medical student. But what is he doing here? Clutching the edge of the curtain, he obviously wonders whether to enter or not. Will he choose to initiate himself into the mysteries of the flesh, or will he close the curtains on this den of iniquity?

The only figure who remains completely unmoved by what is going on around him is the central figure, on account no doubt of the plate of water-melon and *porrón* of red wine which occupy his attention. This imperturbable client is a sailor – indeed, what could be more predictable in a harbour-town brothel? – and Picasso has obviously enjoyed the meticulous execution of his handsome uniform with its large crescent-shaped collar and the sailor's pompom-hat which sits immovably on his head. Picasso also gives us a more brutal depiction of him, where he appears bare-chested, divested of his operetta-style costume, rolling a cigarette while he awaits his turn. The artist obviously wavers over the characterization of his model, for first he draws the slightly coarse features of a mature man, thick-necked and square-jawed, wearing a sulky expression. Then he draws a full-length portrait of a slight figure with a quizzical smile. He also appears on a very fine page of pen-and-ink studies with the features of a dreamy young man who closely resembles Pablo Picasso. Every now and then, the features of the two men fuse – the same classical profile, the same wide-open eyes, the same high forehead with strands of boyish hair. One no longer knows which is the sailor and which the student, nor how to distinguish between Virtue and Vice, since they assume the same guise.

During that month of March 1907, Picasso had not yet 'discovered' African art, being still under the spell of Pre-Christian Iberian art, recently revealed to him by an exhibition at the Louvre devoted to the archaeological digs at Cerro de los Santos. For a time, the Bateau-Lavoir studio was itself to harbour two of these rough stone heads, unluckily acquired from a crook who passed himself off as Apollinaire's secretary. One of them, a male head, was to inspire the flatly incised eyes, the large rimmed ears and the short fringe of the two clients of the Carrer d'Avinyo brothel. The female faces also undergo this primitive stylization. Without pity for our young ladies, whom he has already endowed with an athletic frame that calls their gender into question, the artist's pencil rounds on their delicate little faces, which become swallowed up by huge eyes surmounted by perfectly arched eyebrows extending into enormous noses, prefiguring the notorious 'wedges of Brie' which were to cause such a commotion. Were it not for their long tresses, nothing would distinguish them from their chance companions. Like them, they have that aura of sorrowful dignity – with their impassive faces and absent gaze – which Gertrude Stein so admired.

This atmosphere of melancholia which seems to afflict all the characters, together with the emblematic presence of the two men surrounded by symbolic objects (vanities or sexual substitutes?), all suggest that beneath the trivial story-telling element lies an allegorical meaning. Would Picasso (although one has difficulty in imagining him in a moralizing role) have seen in this work, 'a sort of charade on the wages of sin', a *memento mori* symbolized by the pair formed by the student (Virtue) and the sailor (Vice), as Alfred Barr tentatively suggested? Leo Steinberg, for his part, prefers to see the student holding the book as a symbol of knowledge, 'a man apart . . . condemned for not entering'. When, during the progress of the work, the two men disappear, and with them the anecdotal element, leaving the stage to the women, this moralizing intention is spirited away in favour of formal experiments renewed by the discovery of primitive art forms. This 'exorcism-painting', can now be plainly seen as what it has in fact never ceased to be – a brutal sexual metaphor.

Although this sketchbook recounts a scheme which never saw the light of day, it remains nonetheless unforgettable. At the turn of every page, the emotive power of its beauty takes one's breath away. You thought you were entering a vulgar *salon* and, somewhat disconcerted, you discover solemn faces, fresh flowers in a vase, a young bitch feeding her litter and the obsessive presence of a skull. . . .

BRIGITTE LEAL

Sketchbook

March 1907, Paris

Black chalk, black ink, coloured crayons, pastel and *charcoal*
h. 19.3 cm, w. 24.2 cm
Paris, Musée Picasso

Rectangular sketchbook, bound along the shorter edge, comprising fifty pages of pale-buff paper, cotton-stitched, with buff cloth-covered boards. All the sheets (except the verso of sheet 28) have been worked, either vertically or horizontally, the right way up or with the sketchbook inverted, on recto and verso alike. Apart from the two charcoal studies, the great majority of the drawings are in black chalk, a number are in pen and ink, and a few are heightened with other media. The inside front cover is inscribed in ink, in Picasso's handwriting. The inside back cover also features a drawing in both chalk and black ink. Tucked into the back of the sketchbook between the last page and the back cover, a small piece of paper of a different type to that of this sketchbook bears a geometrical sketch – a square overlaid with a circle drawn in black chalk as well as an inscription in Spanish in Picasso's own hand: '*Un felpudo abajo del cuadro entre las cortinas de los lados*' ('A mat at the base of the painting between the curtains at the sides').

In the following list, the numbers refer to the inventory numbers usually found on the bottom right-hand corner of the recto pages in the sketchbook, following the oblique stroke (1063/1, etc.) **R** *stands for recto,* **V** *for verso.*

Inside front cover. Inscription: 'From Fèvre et Cie, 237 rue Lafayette, telephone no. 403-62 / Laigneville bed (white, soft stone) 45 F per cubic metre / Buisson Richard bed – 38 [F] / At the St-Denis quarry, Seine et Oise, from Daubin Frère or / from Arazin / St-Denis quarry bed pale yellowish stone / and soft 36 F per cubic metre / For such purchases it is always preferable to choose a / sample that has been damaged in cutting by the quarriers, in which case / the dealer only charges for the solid cube [that can be cut out] of the piece.'

1R Study for the *demoiselle* squatting on the right, seen from the back: seated nude and head
charcoal

1V Study for the sailor: head and shoulders and pompom hat
black chalk

2R Compositional study with seven figures: five *demoiselles*, the sailor and the medical student
black chalk

2V Study for the sailor: head
black chalk

3R Compositional study with one figure: the *demoiselle* squatting on the right, seen from the back, and the still-life
black chalk

3V Study for the sailor: head
black chalk

4R Study for the *demoiselle* with upraised arms: half-length nude figure with upraised arms
black chalk

4V Study for the *demoiselle* squatting on the right, seen from the back: head with long hair, seen from the back
black chalk

5R Compositional study with two figures: the *demoiselle* standing on the right, the *demoiselle* with upraised arms; female head and sketch of a figure obscured by a wash of ink
black chalk and ink wash

5V Study for the sailor: seated man rolling a cigarette
black chalk

6R Compositional study with seven figures: five *demoiselles*, the medical student and the sailor
black chalk

6V Page of studies for the *demoiselle* with upraised arms, the *demoiselle* standing on the right and the still-life: standing nudes and half-length nudes with upraised arms; hands parting curtains; slices of watermelon
black chalk

7R Study for the seated *demoiselle*, seen from the front: seated nude, legs crossed
black chalk

7V Study for the *demoiselle* squatting on the right, seen from the back: profile of a woman
black chalk

8R Study for the medical student: nude in profile with arm raised; ears
pen and black ink, black chalk

8V Compositional study with seven figures: five *demoiselles*, the medical student and the sailor
black chalk

9R Compositional study with five figures: three *demoiselles*, the medical student and the sailor. Drawn over a pen-and-ink sketch of a pot of flowers on a table-cloth
black chalk

9V Study for the *demoiselle* squatting on the right, seen from the back: seated nude, seen from the back
black chalk

10R Study for the still-life: slices of water-melon on a plate
pastel and black chalk

10V Study for the medical student: nude in profile with arm raised
black chalk

11R Obliterated drawing
black chalk

11V Page of studies for the medical student and the sailor: half-length figure of a man with arm raised, holding a skull; heads and shoulders of a sailor
black chalk

12R Compositional study with two figures and study of square shape: the standing *demoiselle* in profile and the seated *demoiselle*, seen from the front
charcoal
drawn at right-angles over a study for the *demoiselle* squatting on the right, seen from the back
pen and black ink

12V Study for the *demoiselle* standing on the right: nude in profile drawing aside a curtain
black chalk

13R Study for the *demoiselle* squatting on the right, seen from the back: seated nude with legs apart
pen and black ink

13V Study for the seated *demoiselle*, seen from the front: nude with drapery
black chalk

14R Study for the *demoiselle* squatting on the right, seen from the back: profile of woman with long hair
pen and black ink

14V Compositional study with seven figures: five *demoiselles*, the medical student and the sailor
black chalk

15R Study for the *demoiselle* with upraised arms: nude with upraised arms, seen from the front
black chalk

15V Study for the medical student: hand holding a skull
black chalk

16R Study for the still-life: vases
black chalk

16V Study for the medical student: hand holding a skull
black chalk

17R Study for the still-life: vase
black chalk

17V Study for the medical student: hand holding a skull
black chalk

18R Study for the medical student: man in profile with raised arm, holding a skull
black chalk

18V Compositional study with seven figures: five *demoiselles*, the medical student and the sailor
black chalk

19R Study for the still-life: fruit in a bowl
coloured crayons, pen and black ink

19V Compositional study with six figures: four *demoiselles*, the medical student and the sailor
black chalk

20R Page of studies for the *demoiselle* squatting on the right, seen from the back: seated nude with legs apart, seen from the back; hands
pen and black ink

20V Compositional study with seven figures: five *demoiselles*, the medical student and the sailor
black chalk

21R Page of studies for the sailor: half-length figure, head and shoulders, hand
pen and black ink

21V Compositional study with two figures: the *demoiselle* squatting on the right, seen from the back, the *demoiselle* standing on the right and vase of flowers on a table
black chalk

22R Study for the still-life: bouquet of flowers in a vase and slice of water-melon
black ink, black chalk and gum

22V Compositional study with four figures: the sailor, the *demoiselle* with upraised arms, the *demoiselle* squatting on the right, seen from the back, and the *demoiselle* standing on the right
black chalk

23R Study for the medical student: head and shoulders of a man in profile
black chalk, pen and black ink

23V Studies of nudes, seen from the front
pen and black ink

24R Page of studies: half-length figure of the medical student; seated nude with legs crossed; sketches of nudes and animals
black ink

24V Compositional study with two figures: the *demoiselle* squatting on the right and the *demoiselle* standing on the right
black chalk

25R Study for the medical student: head of a man in profile
black chalk

25V Compositional study with seven figures: five *demoiselles*, the medical student and the sailor
black chalk

26R Study for the still-life: vase of flowers on a table
black chalk
drawn over a sketch of a tablecloth
graphite pencil

26V Study for the *demoiselle* standing on the right(?): head in profile
black chalk

27R Study for the still-life: flowers
pastel and black chalk

27V Study for the still-life: vase of flowers
black chalk

28R Compositional study with seven figures, vertical format: five *demoiselles*, the medical student, the sailor and Fricka
black chalk

28V Blank page

29R Compositional study with seven figures: five *demoiselles*, the medical student and the sailor
black chalk

29V Compositional study with one figure: the seated *demoiselle*, seen from the front, and the still-life
black chalk

30R Studies for the medical student: man in profile holding a book
black chalk

30V Study for the sailor: head of a man
black chalk

31R Studies of legs
black chalk

31V Study for the seated *demoiselle*, seen from the front: head of a woman
black chalk

32R Studies for the *demoiselle* with upraised arms: half-length nudes with upraised arms, seen from the front, and standing nudes with upraised arms, seen from both the front and the back
black chalk

32V Study for the medical student: head of a man in profile
black chalk

33R Page of studies for the *demoiselle* with upraised arms and the *demoiselle* standing behind the seated *demoiselle*, seen from the front
black chalk

33V Study for the medical student: head of a man in profile
black chalk

34R Study for the *demoiselle* standing behind the seated *demoiselle*, seen from the front: standing nude, one hand resting on the back of the armchair
black chalk

34V Study for the still-life: vase of flowers
black chalk

35R Study for the medical student: head of a man in profile
black chalk

35V Study for the still-life: vase of flowers on a table
black chalk

36R Study for the medical student: head of a man in profile
black chalk

36V Study for the *demoiselle* squatting on the right, seen from

the back: seated nude with long hair, seen from the back
black chalk

37R Study for the *demoiselle* standing behind the seated *demoiselle* on the left: half-length figure of a woman
black chalk

37V Study for the medical student: man in profile with arm raised, holding a skull, head in profile
black chalk

38R Studies of hands
black chalk

38V Study for the *demoiselle* squatting on the right, seen from the back: seated nude with long hair, seen from the back
black chalk

39R Study for the medical student: hand holding a book
black chalk

39V Studies of feet
black chalk

40R Page of studies: foot, *porrón* and slices of water-melon on a table
black chalk

40V Compositional study with two figures: the medical student and the *demoiselle* standing behind the seated *demoiselle*, seen from the front
black chalk

41R Study for the still-life: *porrón* and slices of water-melon on a table
black chalk

41V Study for the *demoiselle* squatting on the right, seen from the back: head of a woman in profile
black chalk

42R Study for the still-life: slices of water-melon on a plate
black chalk

42V Page of studies: hanging baskets of flowers and legs of the medical student
black chalk

43R Page of studies for the *demoiselle* standing behind the seated *demoiselle*, on the left, and the medical student
black chalk

43V Study for the seated *demoiselle*, seen from the front: head of a woman with long hair
black chalk

44R Study for the *demoiselle* standing behind the seated *demoiselle*, seen from the front: half-length nude, and standing nude with one hand resting on the back of an armchair
black chalk

44V Study for the sailor: head of a man
black chalk

45R Study for the medical student: half-length figure of a man in profile holding a book
black chalk, black ink and coloured crayon

45V Man standing on a ladder in an interior (the Bateau-Lavoir studio?)
black chalk

46R Page of studies for the *demoiselle* squatting on the right, seen from the back: seated nude with legs apart, seen from the front; and square compositional study with one figure: the *demoiselle* squatting on the right, seen from the back, and the still-life
black chalk

46V Study for the sailor: standing man seen from the front
black chalk

47R Study for the *demoiselle* squatting on the right, seen from the back: seated nude with legs apart, seen from the front
black chalk

47V Study for the *demoiselle* squatting on the right, seen from the back: head of a woman with long hair in profile
black chalk

48R Study for the *demoiselle* with upraised arms: standing nudes with upraised arms
black chalk

48V Study for the *demoiselle* squatting on the right, seen from the back: seated nude with long hair, seen from the back
black chalk

49R Study for the *demoiselle* with upraised arms: nudes with upraised arms
black chalk

49V Bitch feeding her young (Fricka)
black chalk

50R Study for the *demoiselle* with upraised arms: standing nude with upraised arms, arms and doodle
black chalk, pen and black ink

50V Bitch feeding her young (Fricka)
black chalk

Inside back cover. Bitch feeding her young (Fricka) and geometrical sketch
black chalk, pen and black ink

The Sketchbook

chez Fevre et Cie 237 Rue Lafayette   N° Telephone 403-62

Banc Laigneville (pierre blanche et tendre 45f le metre cube

Banc Buisson Richard ———— 38

A carrière St Denis S. et O.   chez Daubin frère ou

chez Arazin

Banc carrière St Denis   pierre legerement jaunat

et tendre 36f le metre cu

Pour ces sortes de achat il est toujours preferable de choi
la pierre sur place. parce que l'on peut choisir un
echantillon ébréché à la taille par les carriers. dans ce cas
le marchand ne fait payer que le cube réel du morceau

1063/1 z26 100-101

1063/3 . 226.93

1063/5 z 26.9 2

106316

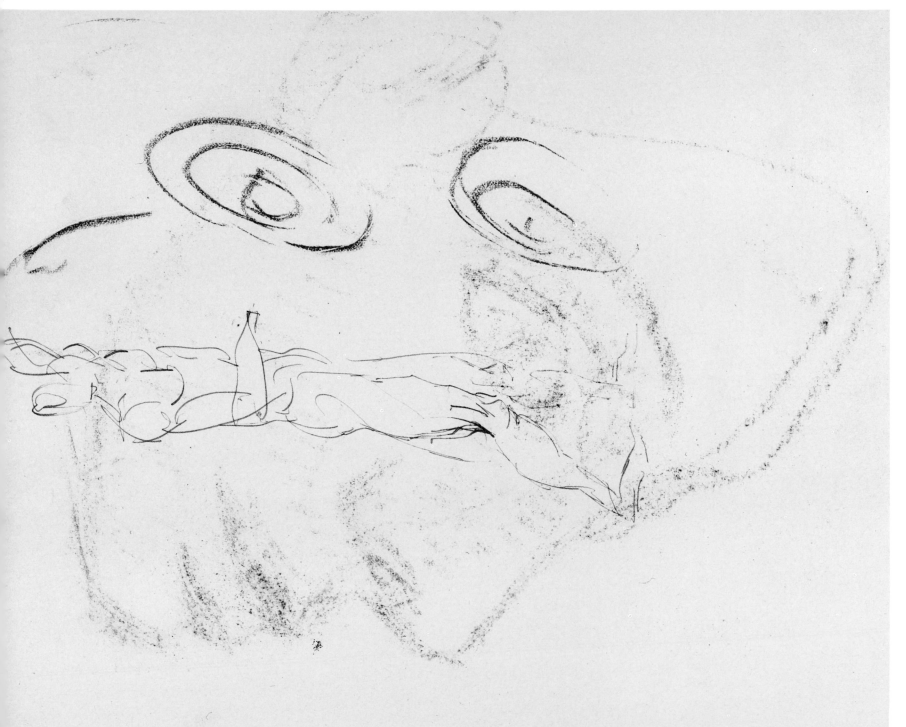

2262091   1063/8

z 26 n°90   1063/9

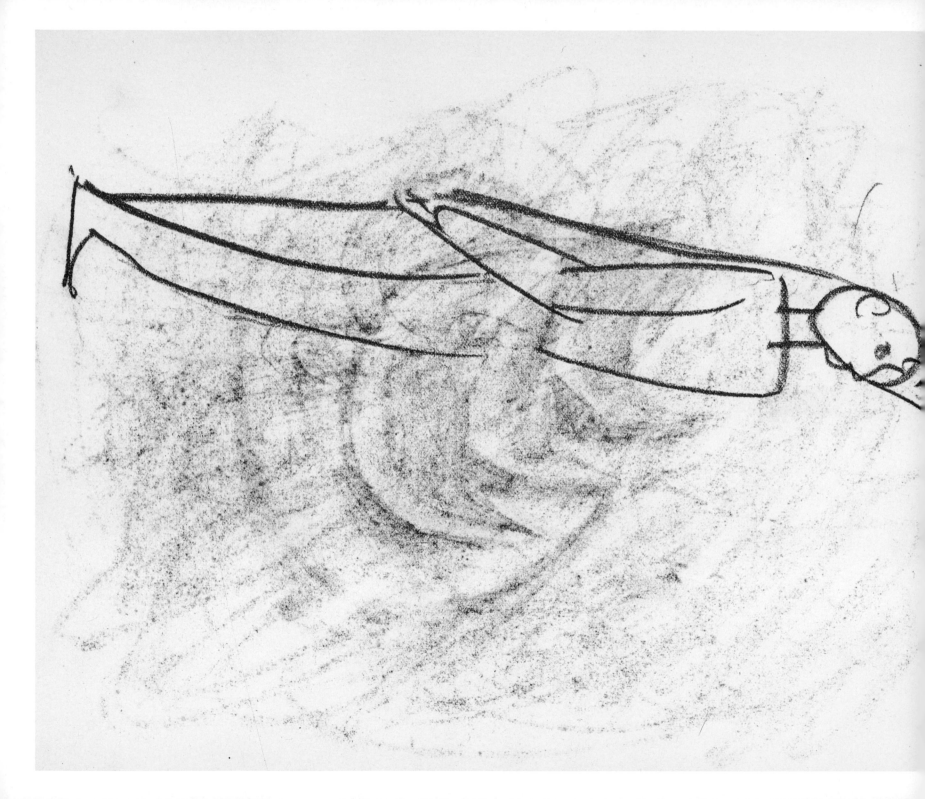

7 26.86   1063/11

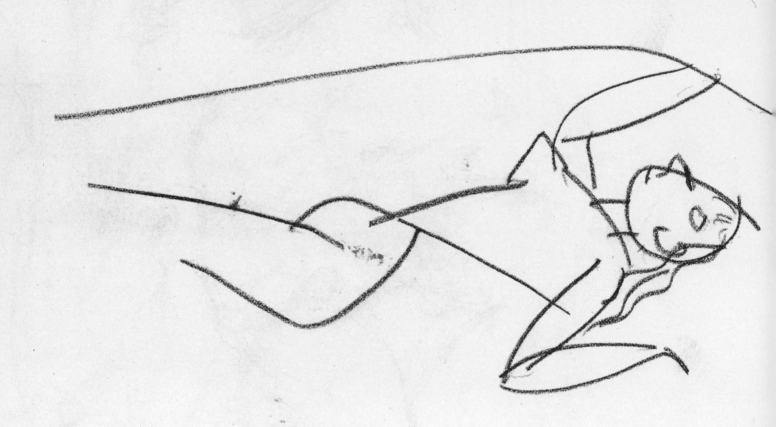

z 26.80 et 85   1063/13

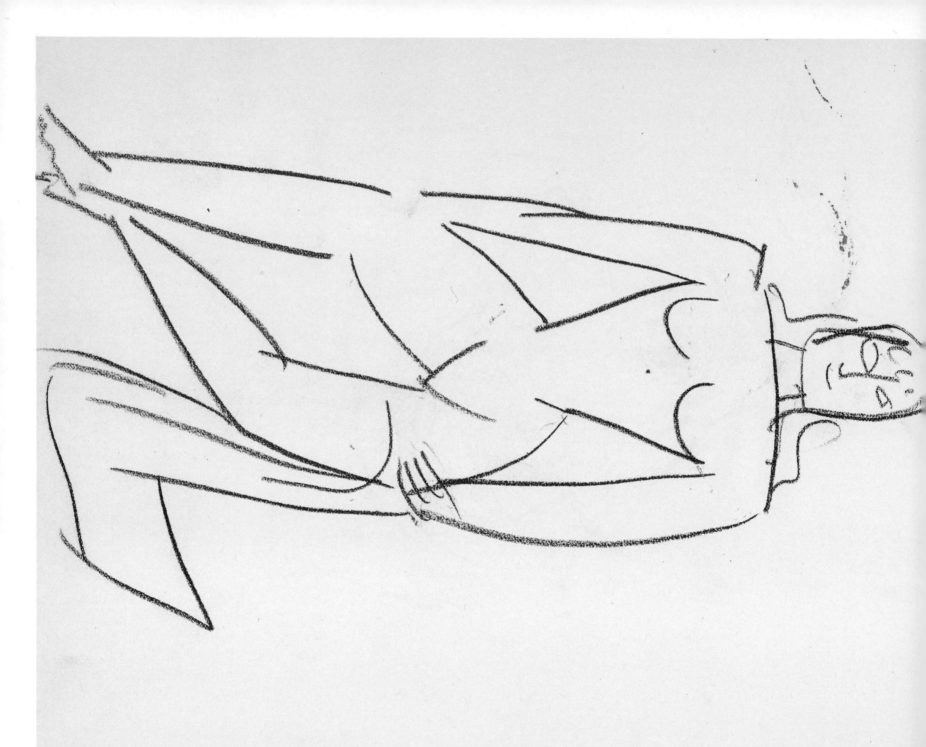

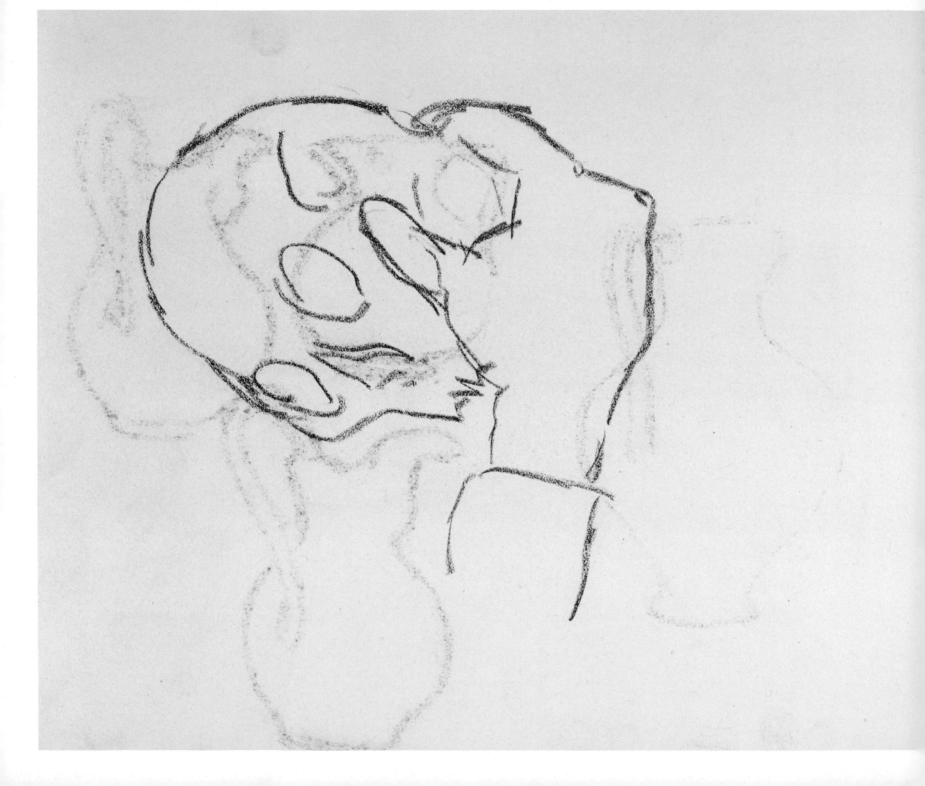

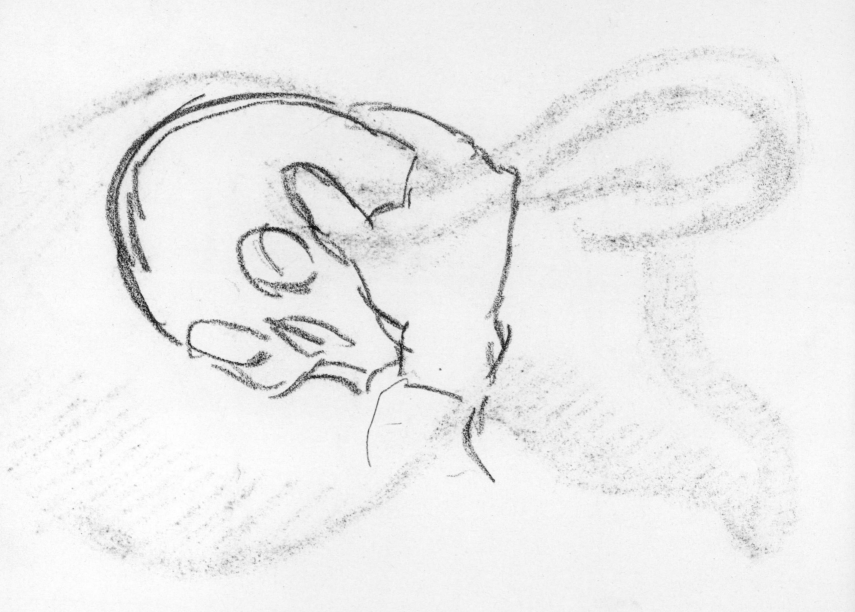

1063/17

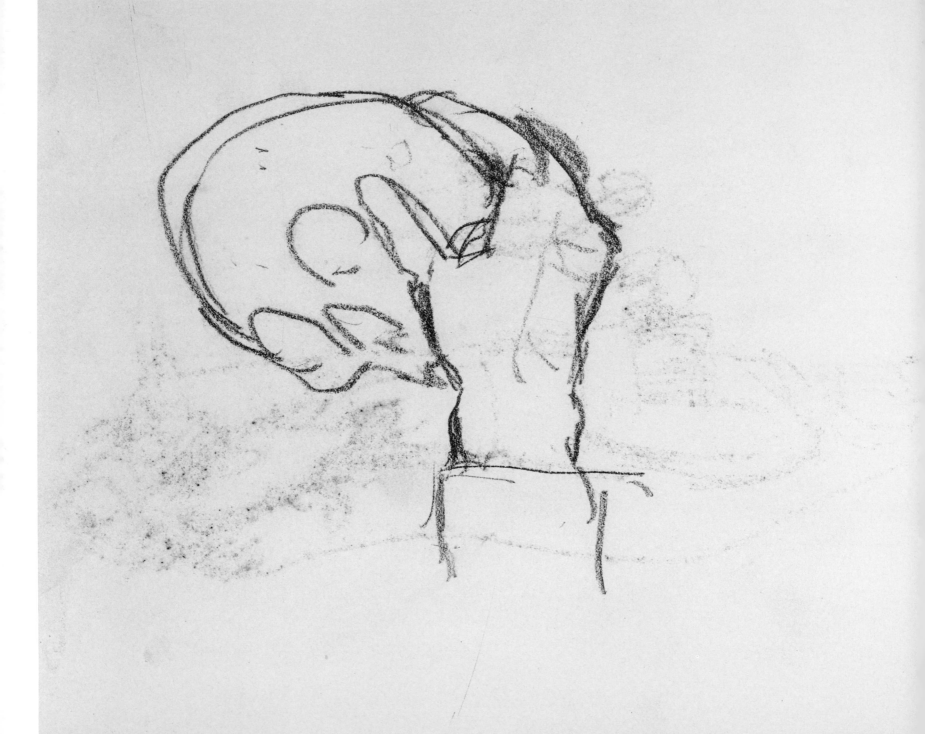

26.7.73   1083/18

z 26.65.69   1063/20

22.6.41   1063/21

726.68   1063/22

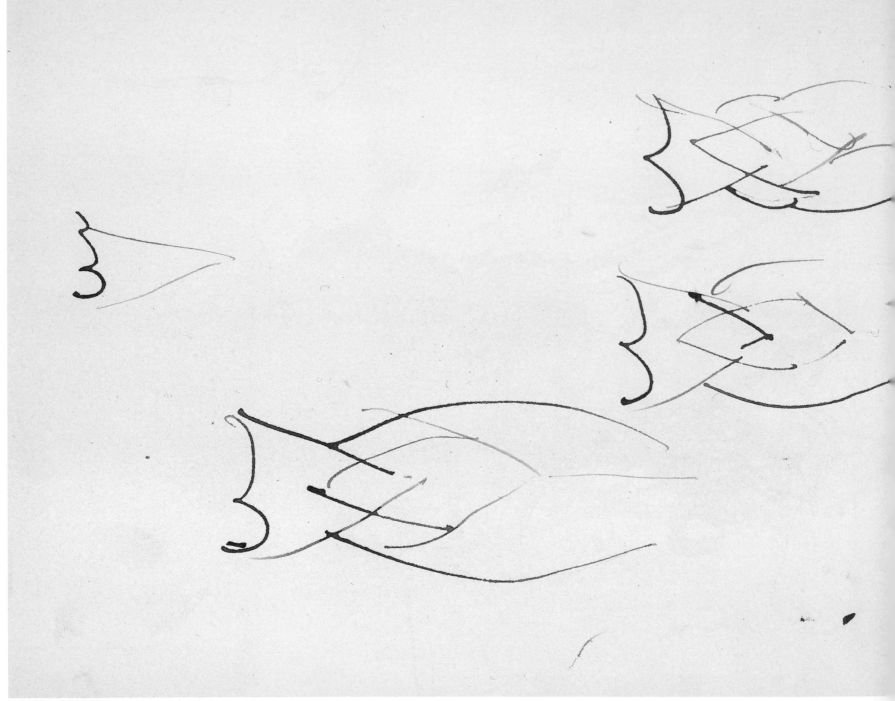

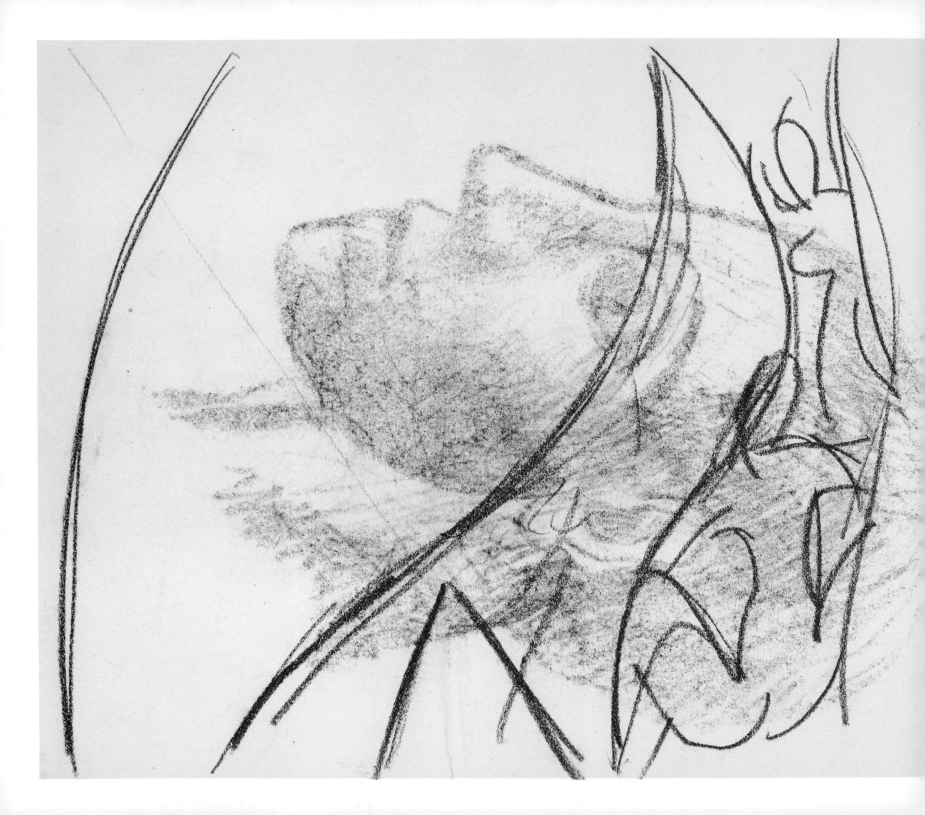

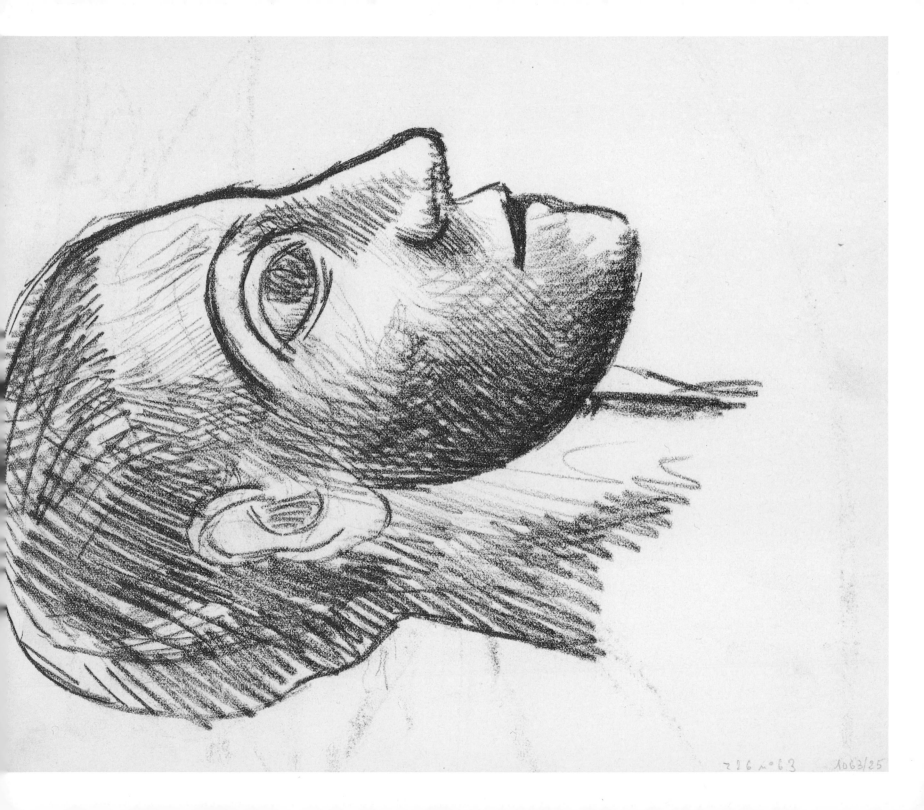

226 n°63   1063/25

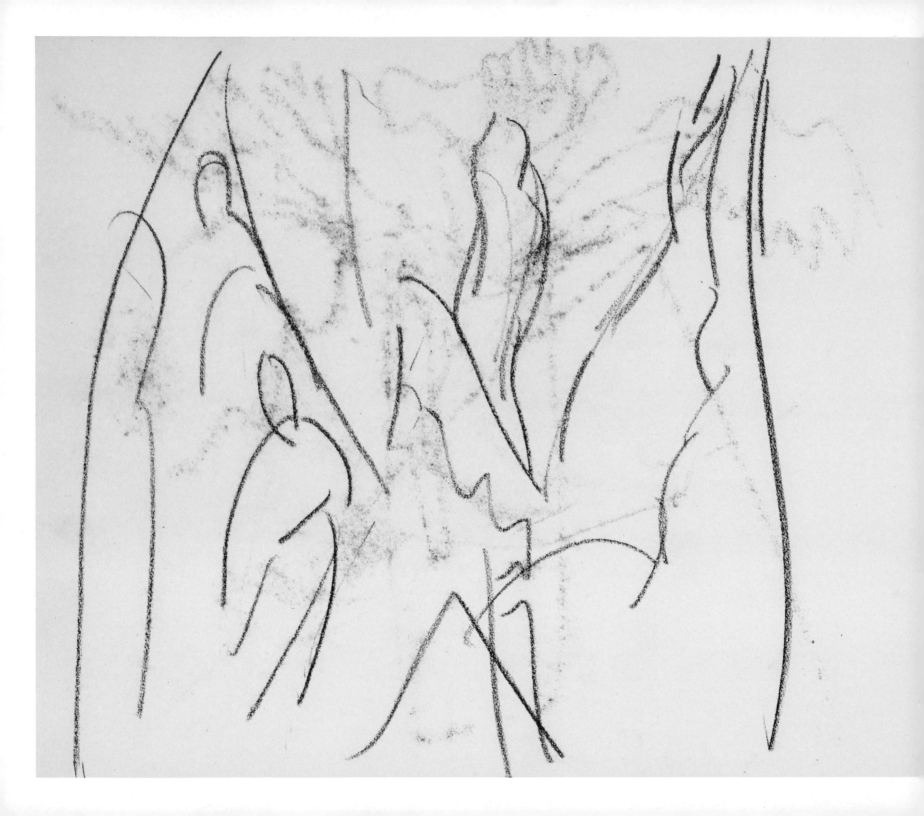

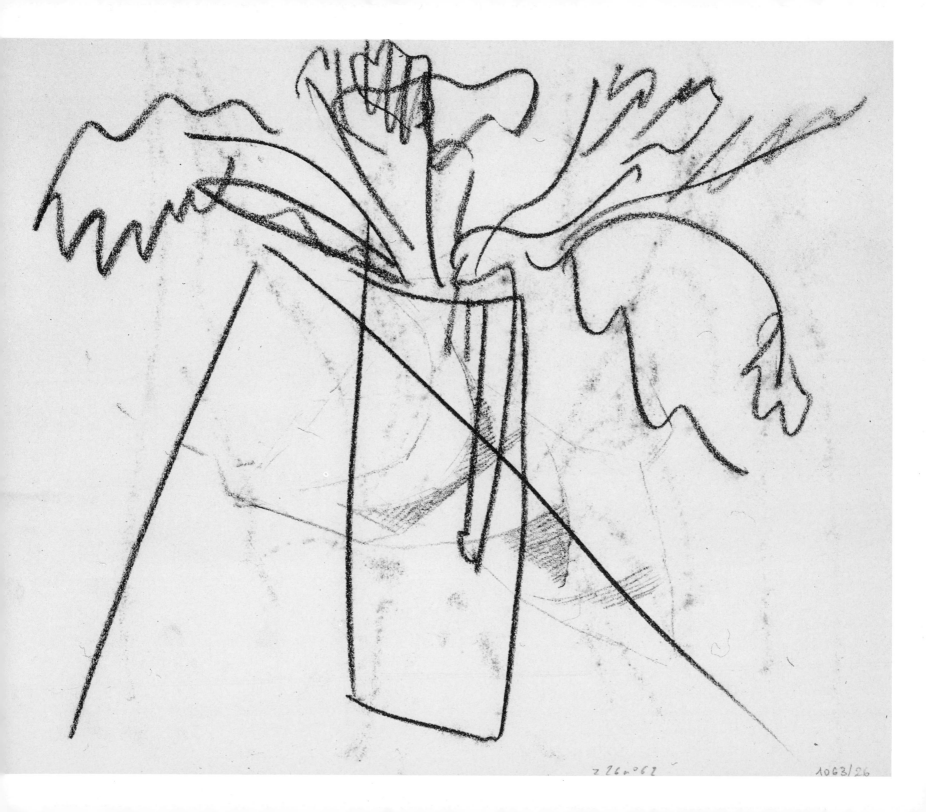

z 26v062   1063/26

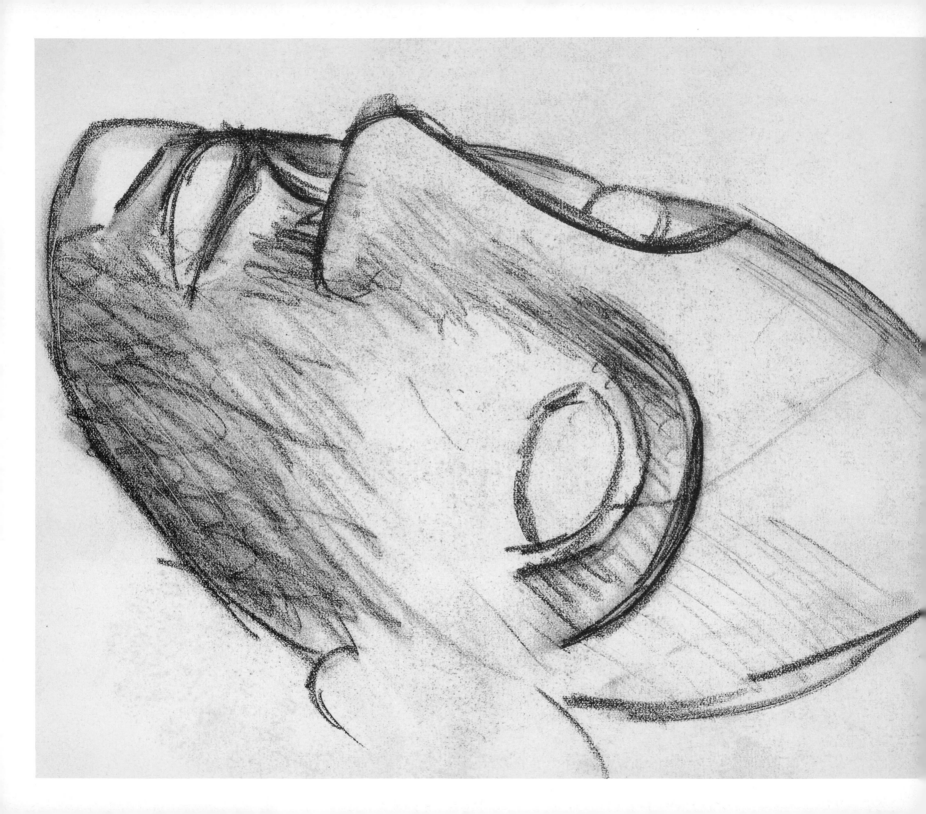

1063/27

Z 26 v 64

1063/28

1063/28

1063/29   226·59

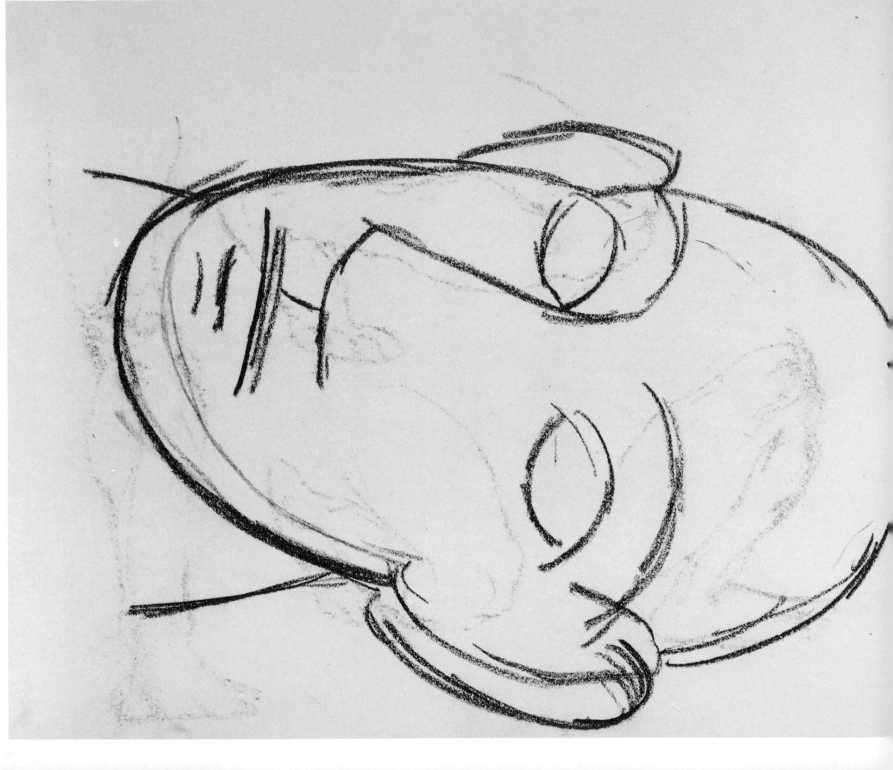

1063/31
226. 56.60

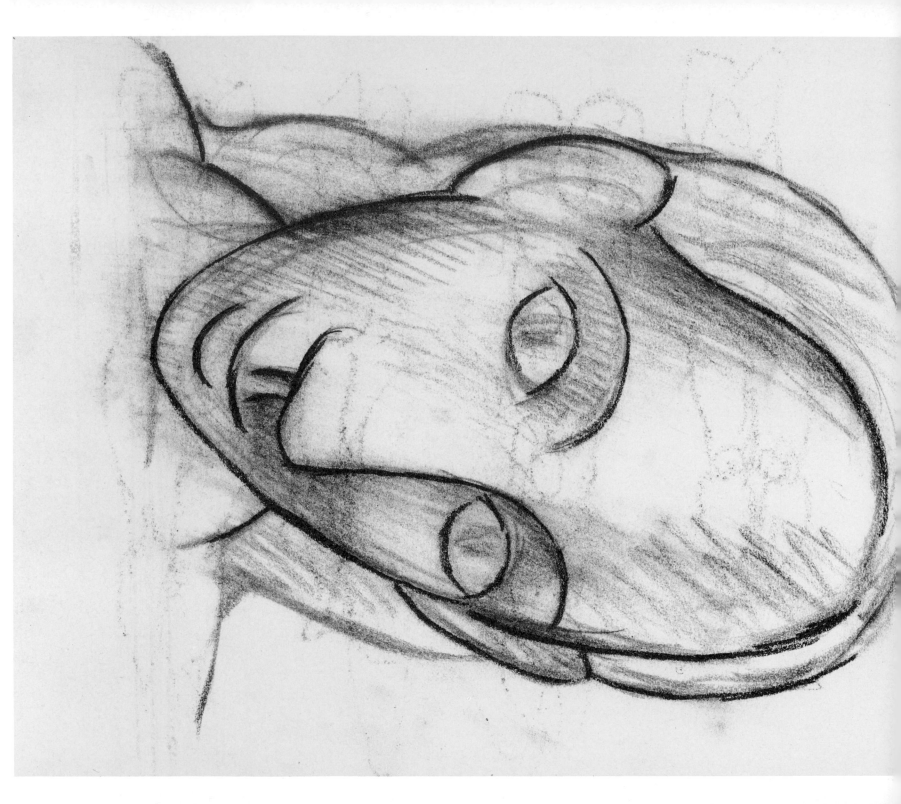

226-55a58   1063/32

1063/34 226.52.53

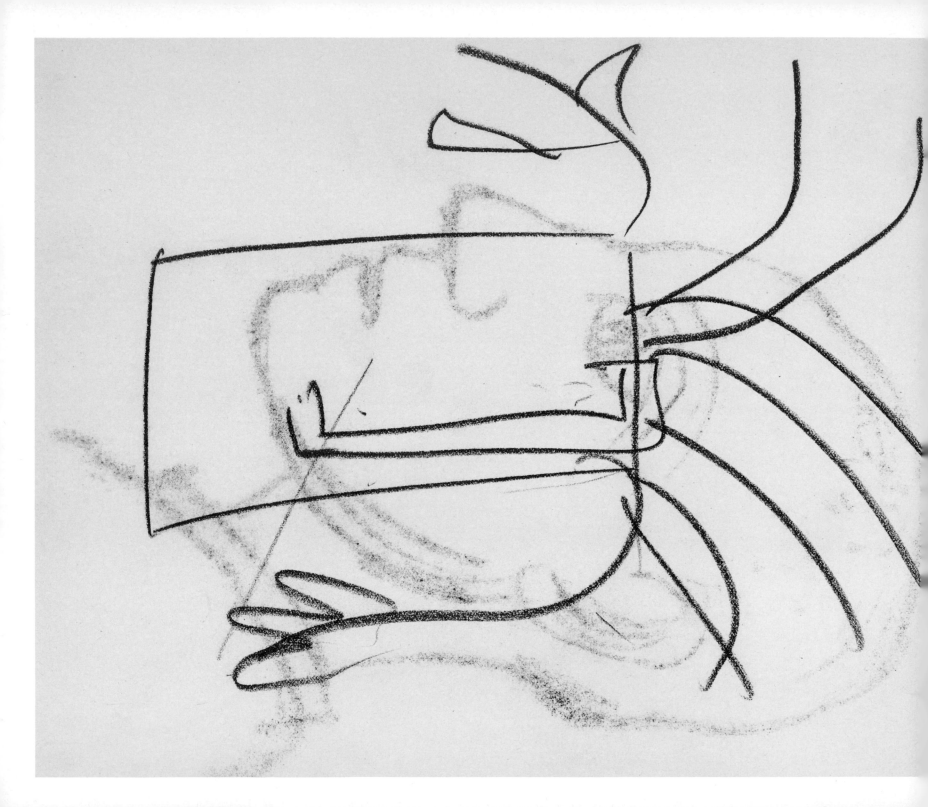

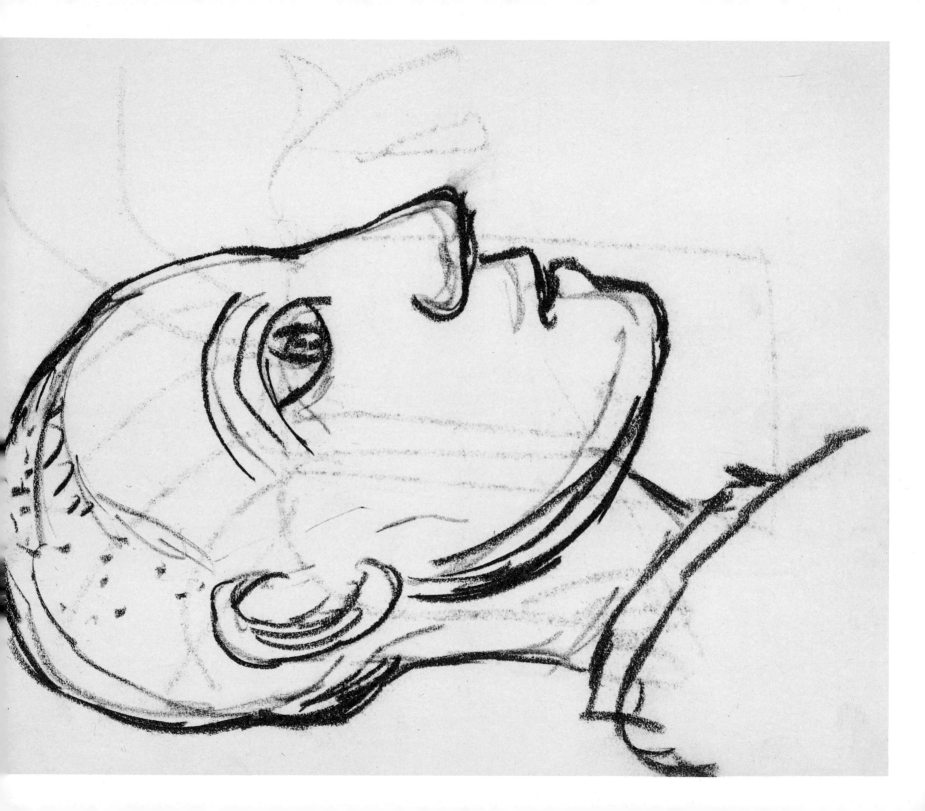

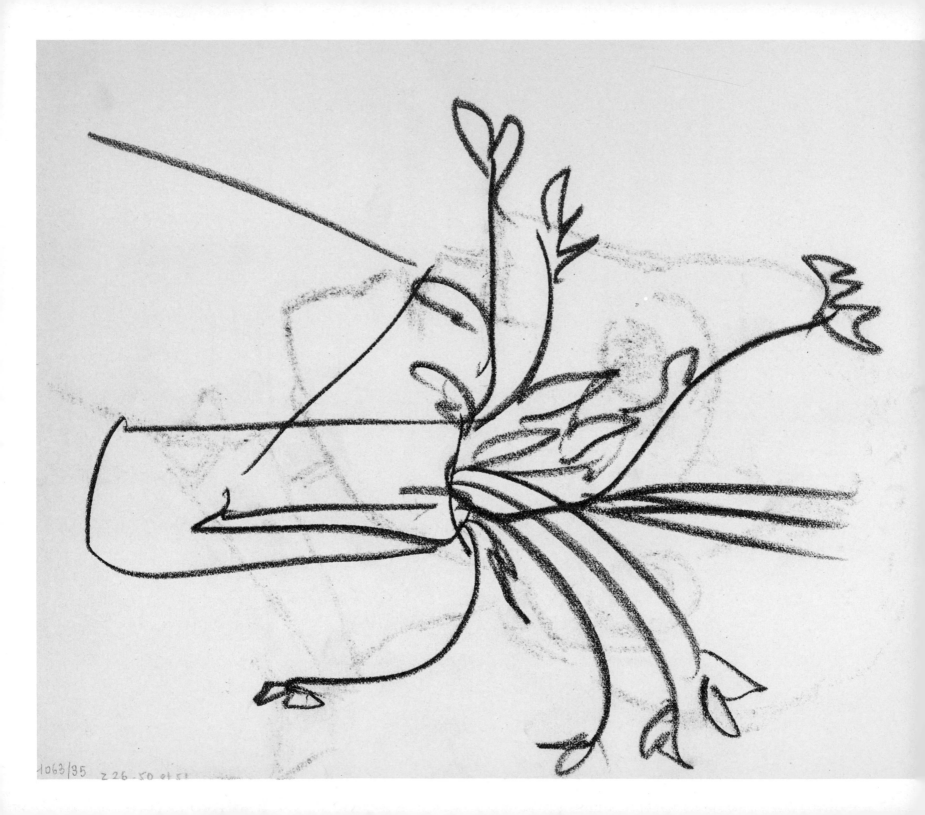

1063/35   z26-50 et 51

137 226.45.46

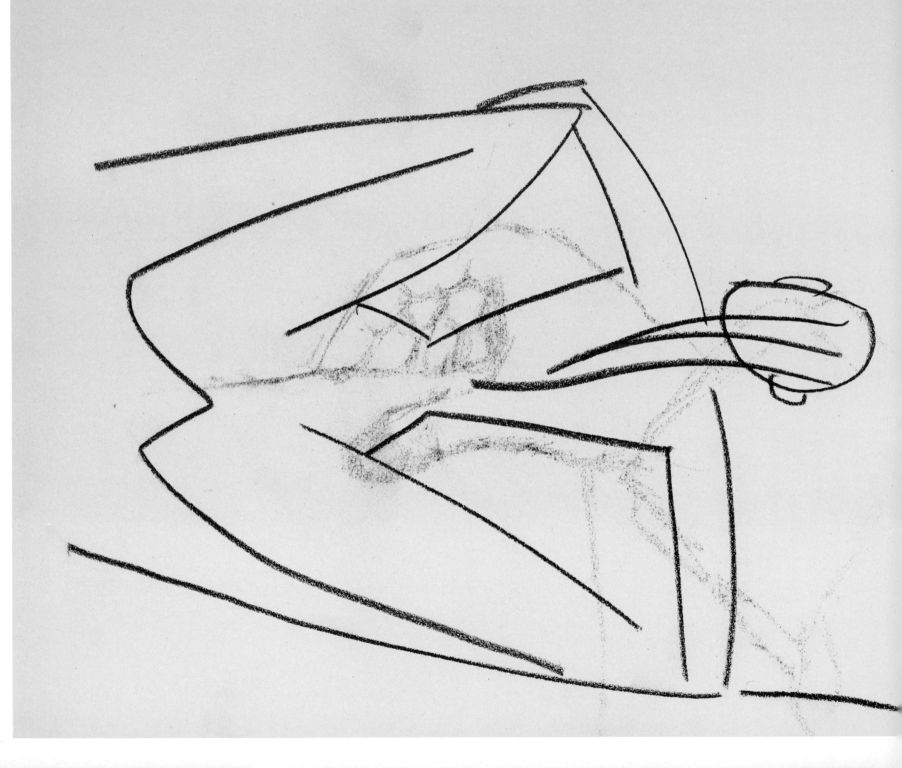

1063/39   Z 26·42·43

226.38.41   1063/40

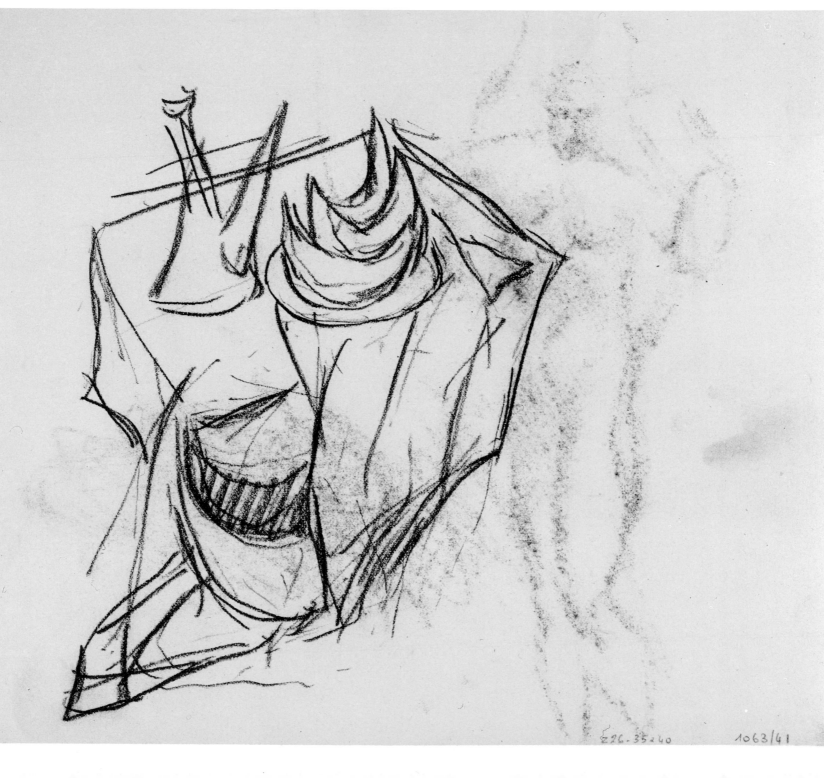

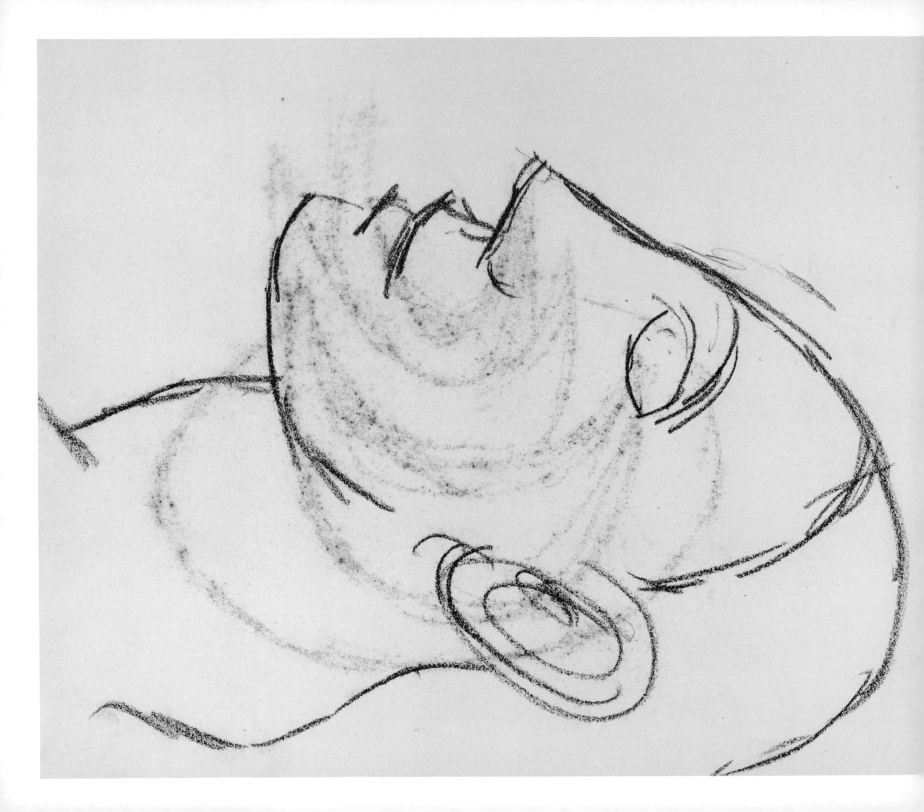

226. 30×34   1063/44

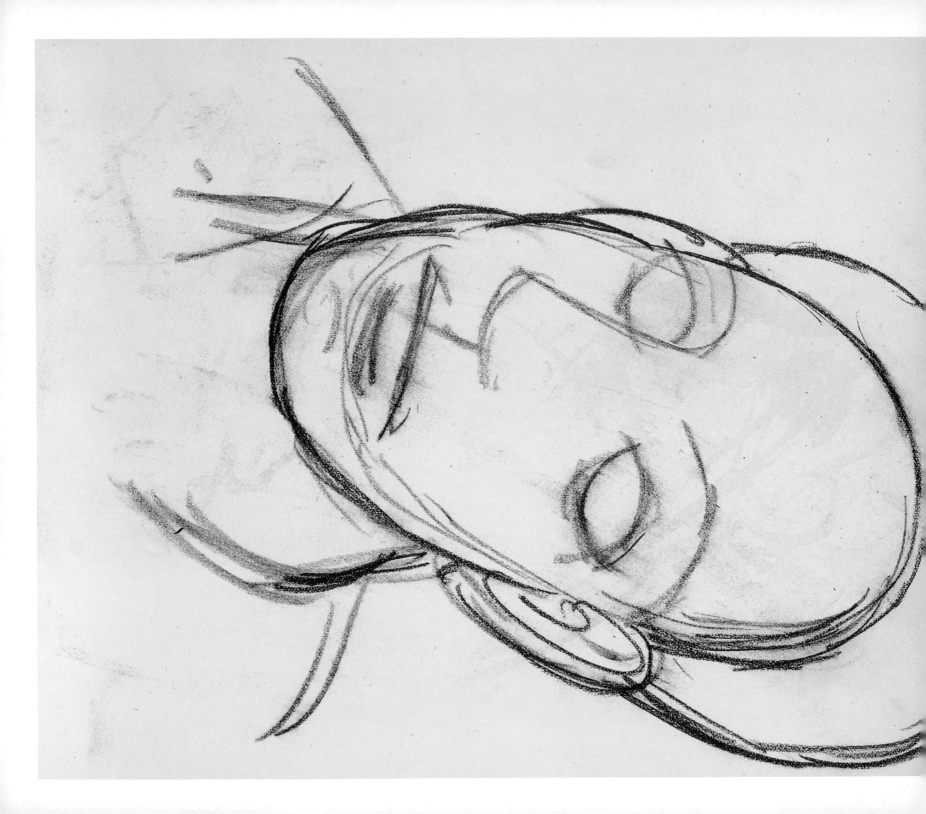

226 - 27 x 21   1063/45

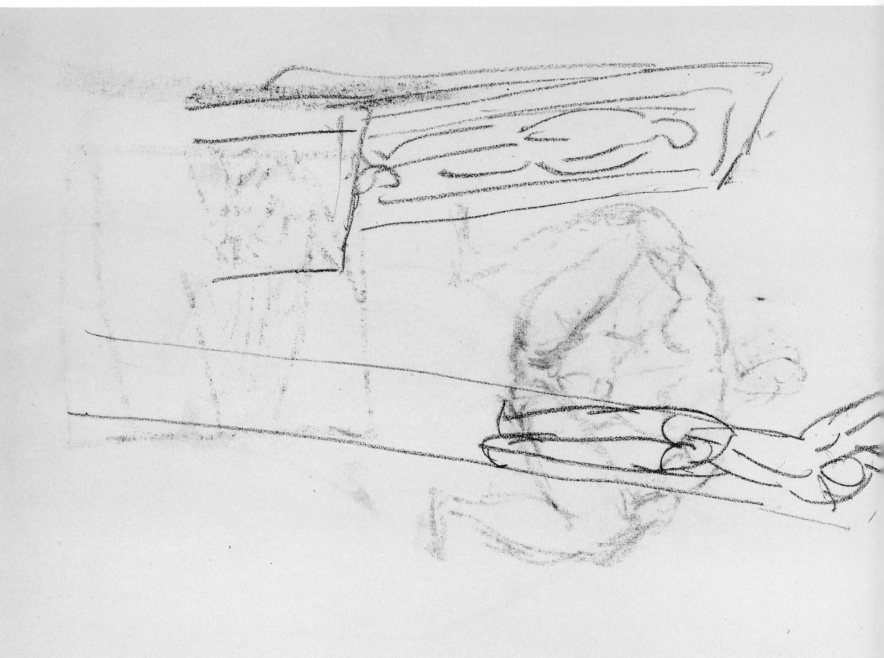

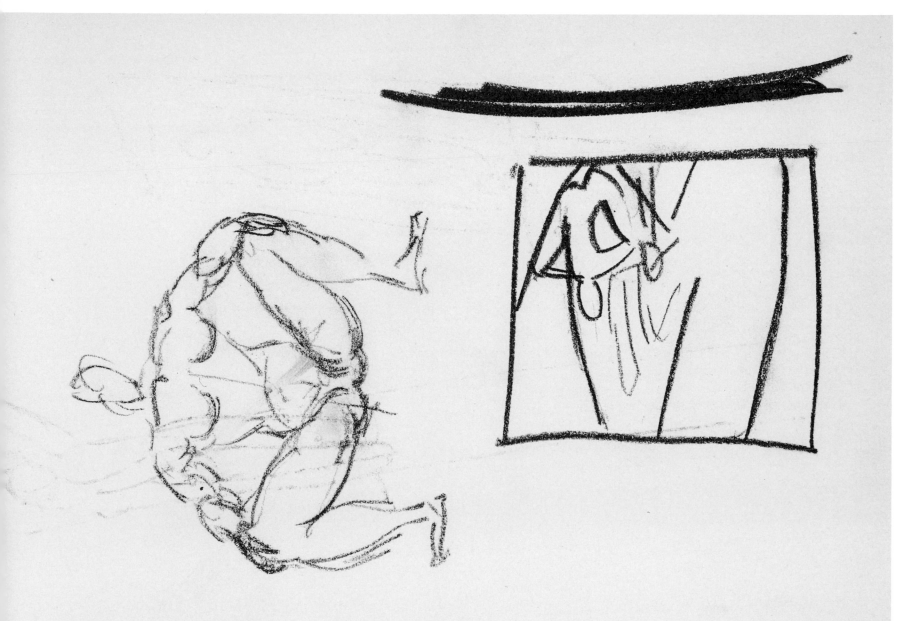

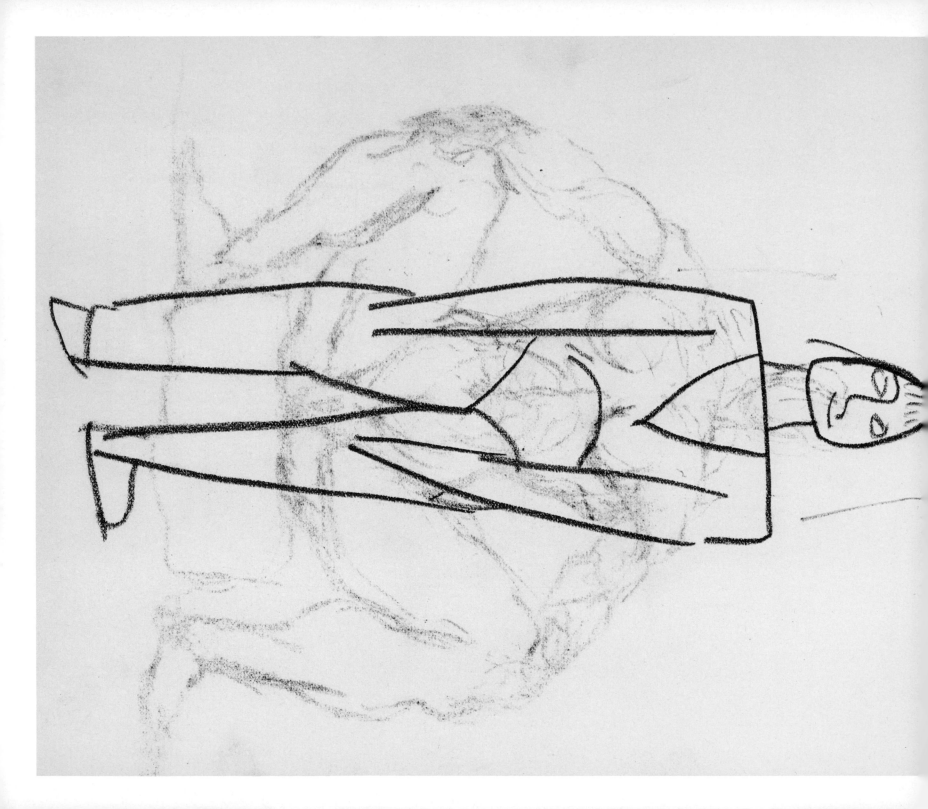

z26·33 et 26   1063/47

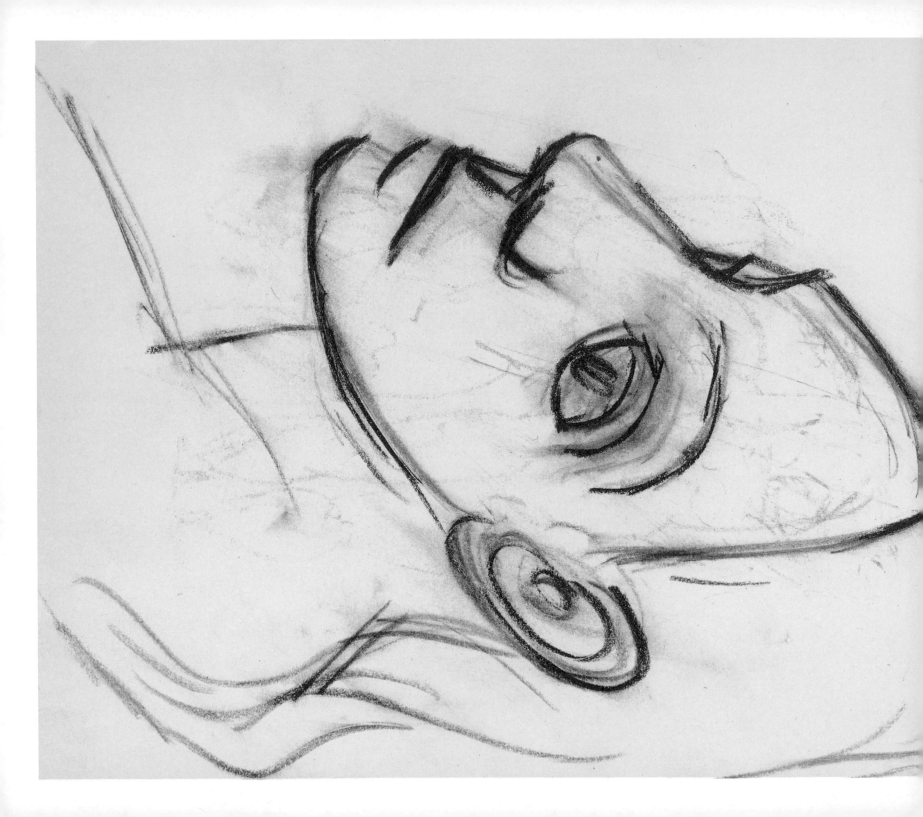

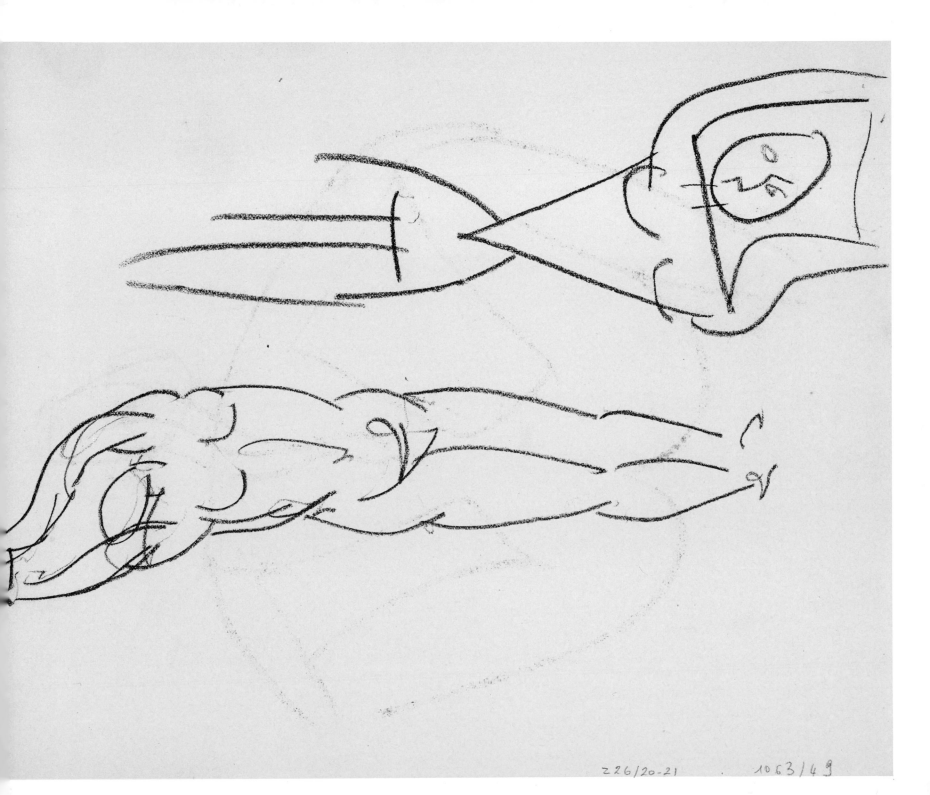

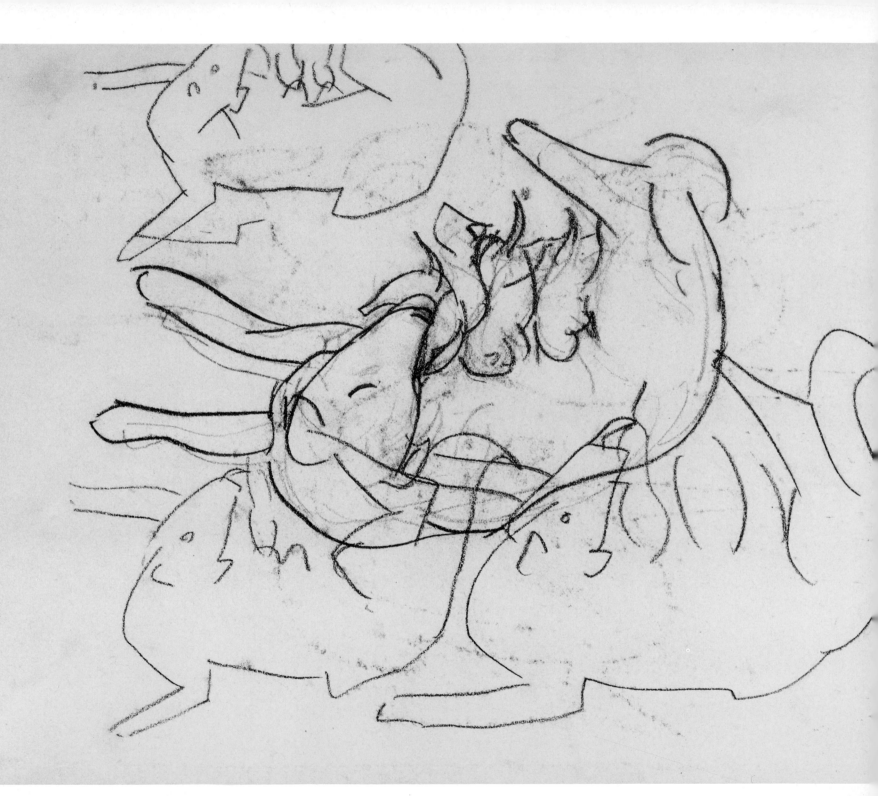

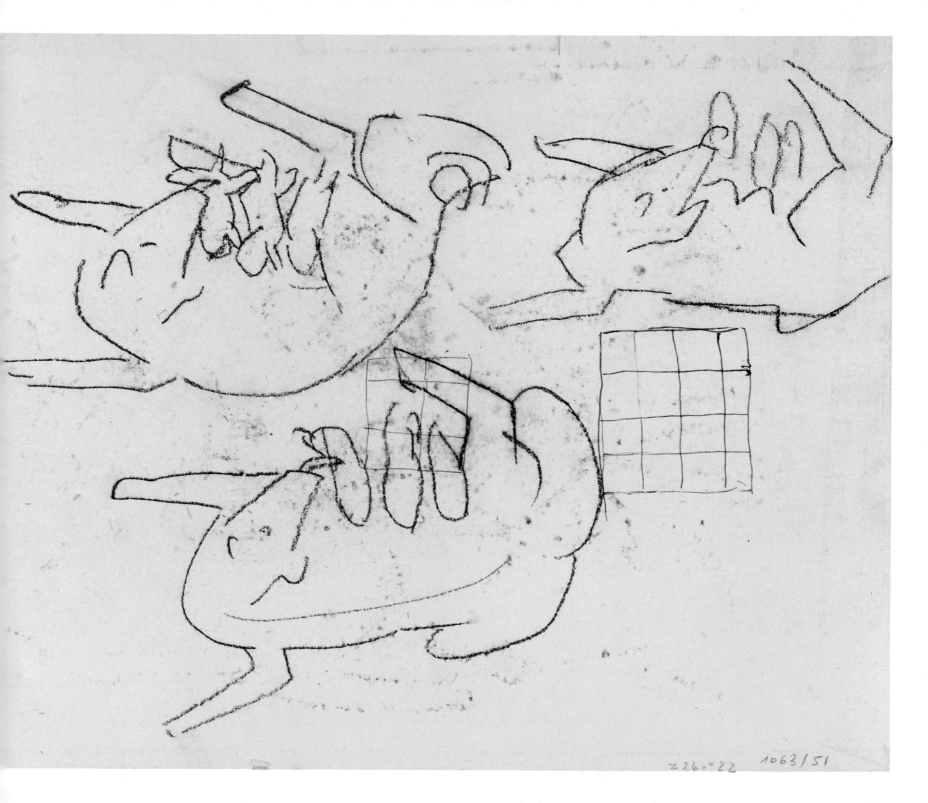